CROSSING
THE
CHASM

MICHAEL T. CONKLIN

ISBN 979-8-89526-286-3 (paperback)
ISBN 979-8-89526-287-0 (digital)

Christian Faith Publishing
832 Park Avenue
Meadville, PA 16335
www.christianfaithpublishing.com

Printed in the United States of America

I chose to write this because it was truly impressed upon my heart; it was almost as if I couldn't escape the calling to put these thoughts into words and write the words down!

The unshakable thought and consideration that kept resurfacing was the lives of the rich man, Lazarus, and Abraham in the book of Luke 16:19–31.

Please let us think about this for a moment: the rich man, Lazarus, and Abraham are in what I will call the afterlife. In the afterlife, or death as some people call it, these three men are able to communicate. Furthermore, it states in the book of Luke that the rich man could actually see Abraham far away, with Lazarus by his side.

Then the rich man called out to Abraham, saying, "Father Abraham, have pity on me and send Lazarus to dip the tip of his finger in water and cool my tongue because I am in agony in this fire."

Wow, really? No kidding, this is a major aha moment for me because they are not dead! They can see, hear, and speak. Dead people can't speak—thankfully, at least not to me!

Now it's not only a major aha moment and a real eye-opener but also brings me a great deal of peace and gives me hope because another thought and realization I'm having is that this story, or biblical account, as well as our present-day lives, predates or are before the second coming of the Savior, the Christ or Messiah. So with that in mind, and as I see it, the rich man who is talking and asks for Abraham's help still has a chance—a chance to be saved from the agony he describes and ultimately a reason for hope.

A chance and a hope for eternal life.

Why should the rich man have hope, and how does he still have a chance at eternal life? Well, friends, dear brothers and sisters, allow me to explain what I've experienced.

In my life, there have been times, situations, and circumstances that I got myself into, and the only way out, the only solution, was for me to humble myself and ask God, our heavenly Father, our creator and sustainer, to please help me. But before I even realized that I should or needed to humble myself, my mind and heart were in agony because of my pride, reasoning with and justifying myself in the things I had said or done.

This sounds very much like the state, condition, and situation of the rich man described in the book of Luke. Then finally, when I realized, when I knew I could and should humble myself, I acknowledged that I was wrong. I took responsibility for my behavior in what I had done or failed to do, in what I said or failed to say. However, I must admit, beloved, there have been too many times and for far too long I was ensnared in my pride, blinded by arrogance, and unable to see the error of my ways. But when I did and humbled myself to the point of crying out, "Abba, Holy Father, dear God, please forgive me," and asked for His help, our Holy Father—yes, our Creator and Sustainer—has always been faithful to lift my burden, open doors, and make a way for me, even at times when I truly thought that there was no way!

Now please do not misunderstand me—no, I don't have it down pat, so to speak. Every day I have to work on humbling myself.

Thinking about the rich man in this story or biblical account, it really seems to me that one of his greatest struggles is his pride and thereby his inability to see the error of his ways and humble himself. The reason why I believe this is because of the fact that I also believe everyone has a conscience, and we know we should speak a kind word, lend a helping hand, or extend a bit of generosity.

The rich man described in the book of Luke lived a life of luxury, and that in and of itself is not bad or a sin, as I see it. Moreover, the Bible tells us in Psalm 25:12–13 that God will instruct those who fear Him in the ways they should choose, and they will spend their lives in prosperity. With that in mind, I must say that if we think about and truly consider the Lord our God, we will surely fear Him! This rich man, though, apparently had no fear of the Lord and also seems to lack compassion. What tells me this is the fact that the Bible states in verse 20, "At his gate laid a beggar named Lazarus," and goes on to describe the horrific and unconscionable state of Lazarus, covered in sores and longing to eat what fell from this rich man's table.

For me personally and in my opinion, generosity, compassion, nor pity have to be taught. I believe that our Holy Father speaks to us through His spirit and into our hearts—this is the conscience. Believe me, I am no saint and haven't always listened to or heeded my conscience, but when I don't obey my conscience, I feel bad, and because I don't like or enjoy feeling bad, I make an effort to correct my behavior and do better!

Truly, friends, really, brothers and sisters, the one thing I have noticed and truly love is how wonderful I feel when I do listen to and heed my conscience, the spirit of our loving creator speaking to my heart. Recently, I was in my little apartment—I'm blessed with a studio apartment that has a nice bathroom, kitchenette, and air conditioning. I was sitting at my little table, which is located just at the end of the kitchenette, and I was trying to do some writing when I heard a bunch of noise outside. Honestly, I got frustrated—really, I was not happy. So I got up, pulled the curtain back, and saw a man doing some work, which didn't make me any happier. I work too—construction, maintenance, etc.—but something told me to open the door and offer the man a glass of water, so I did. Then I got the glass of water and gave it to the man working outside my apartment. I closed the door, pulled the curtain back, and after I sat down again to write, I could still hear the work going on, but it didn't bother me. The burden had truly been lifted, and I had peace.

Now please don't be misled or take me the wrong way—I am far from good and, never mind perfect, so don't think that I describe that situation to boast. No, I'm not boasting. I am and do give the glory and credit to our loving God, who does make a way when I am faithful to listen and heed the voice of His spirit speaking to my heart!

Another thought and consideration that comes to mind is how the rich man in the afterlife is suffering and in agony and still so prideful—prideful, I say, because when he calls out to Abraham, he asks Abraham to send Lazarus to dip the tip of his finger in water to cool his tongue. Really, even in that place of torment, he is still so arrogant and prideful that he would ask for Lazarus to help him—not even to request from Lazarus himself but to ask Abraham to send Lazarus.

Lazarus, the very man that laid at his gate hungry, longing for the scraps that fell from his table, suffering with sores, covered in sores, and to the best of my understanding, the rich man not once provided any relief to Lazarus. And it seems that the rich man, even in that place of torment, thinks more highly of himself than Lazarus—he thinks that he is better than Lazarus.

Beloved, the way I see it is, we have the chance and the opportunity to cross the chasm now so I don't end up suffering the agony described by that rich man in the book of Luke! From the time in childhood and until we take our last breath is the time and opportunity to listen to the Holy Spirit speaking to our hearts and heed our consciences! Yes, believe me, I know that it is easier said than done! But why? It seems so simple—just listen and heed my conscience. Well, I think, actually, I believe that we live in a spiritual war. What I don't believe is that my life consists of or is limited to only that which my eyes can see. I say that because, even though I must sleep—the body requires rest—the mind never stops.

Even when I'm sleeping and the body is resting, the mind is working—I dream. In fact, every minute, every hour that I'm awake, thoughts come to mind, and it really seems to me that the brain doesn't stop. However, I also believe that many—maybe even most—of my thoughts and ideas are my own, intentional or self-generated, like "It's a beautiful day," "It would be nice to see so-and-so," or choosing to buy a vehicle. These are one's natural thoughts and desires, like eating my favorite food to deciding what college to attend or enlisting in the military, as I did, and these intentional or self-generated thoughts are really countless. But there are a lot of thoughts and considerations that come to the human mind that are not or weren't intentional or self-generated by the individual.

I truly believe that there are thoughts and considerations that come to the human mind from an outside source. But before we go further or I get too deep, let me ask you to simply sit and relax. Now try not to think—really try to stop the thought process or think of nothing. Me, personally, I have tried but to no avail—I simply couldn't do it. I have learned to slow my mind down and control my thoughts, focusing on positive things and casting out or sweeping away negative ideas, but my mind won't stop—the thought process is constant. In fact, even to stay in the moment, the present, and not get ahead of myself by thinking about later in the day or tomorrow's wants and needs but simply appreciating the moment, requires effort, and it took me a while to achieve.

Really, think about it. To me, it's truly amazing. I was a human brain, the mind that brought technology from the toaster to the microwave oven and the telegraph to smartphones, and much, much more. Wow, right? Now getting back to the thoughts, ideas, and considerations that I'll refer to as unintentional or not self-generated—the thoughts that come to mind that really aren't me, they don't line up with my values, my beliefs, my desires, or my faith! They won't help get me to where I want or need to go in life, nor do they help me achieve my goals, dreams, or objectives that are most important to me! So where do they come from?

Well, the apostle Paul stated in the book of, or letter to, the church in Rome that "I do not do the good I want to do, but the evil I do not want to do," Wow—that helps me a great deal because before I do or even fail to do something, it starts as a thought or an idea in my mind. It would be simple to say that I or we should just control our thoughts, but the truth is, yes, I absolutely need to take captive and control my mind, and the world would be heavenly if we all could. But in reality, it's not that simple, nor is it easy at all! The reason why it is so difficult at times and more complicated than it seems is because to truly control our thoughts and minds requires perseverance, persistence, and hard work! The thought process consists of a great deal of or large percentage of unintentional or not self-generated thoughts. This is why what the apostle Paul stated makes complete sense to me!

This is a man who was chosen by and walked with the Lord, who stated, "The good that I want to do, I don't, but the evil that I don't want to do are the things I do." God have mercy!

Beloved, let me tell you, for me, I do believe in the God of the Bible and the Bible to be the Word of God! However, not everyone does, and that's okay. Some people were born into Muslim families and the religion of Islam, others Judaism, some people were raised in the religion of Hinduism, and others were taught that there is no God and refer to themselves as atheists. But, friends, please know that we are all human beings and struggle with and suffer from the same malady! We are all spirits, learning from and growing in the human experience! Think with me and please consider the caterpillar.

Some are fuzzy, others are smooth, and they come in different colors, but most, if not all, spin or weave a cocoon around themselves and come out a new creation, a butterfly. It's truly amazing to me—I consider it a miracle, really! I've thought about and considered, and now mention, the caterpillar, its life cycle, and the fact that it turns into a butterfly because I believe that life is a cycle. So living in and growing from this human experience is part of our life cycle, and in this human experience, there are many things we have to endure and situations that require us to persevere in order for us to grow into and become who and what we were created to be! How I see it, so to speak, is this: life is for learning and growing, but in order to grow mentally and spiritually, I must—yes, I have to—deal with, decipher my thoughts, and truly control my mind.

And, beloved, you can do it! It happens little by little—it's a process; it doesn't happen overnight, but it does last for the rest of your life! So I consider how the caterpillar moves, how slowly it walks and the little bites it takes, and becomes a new creation. The once-caterpillar is now a beautiful butterfly! So what I must do is consider the thoughts and ideas that come to mind because some are intentional, but others come from and are generated by something or someone outside of me and are of no help to me! So where do these crazy thoughts and ridiculous ideas come from? Again, as Paul stated, "The very things I don't want to do are the things I do," etc. Well, friends, truly, my brothers and sisters, I believe that we live in a spiritual war.

So I must consider what the Bible teaches me about the fall.

He who once was Lucifer and is now Satan, the devil, a fallen angel, was truly beautiful, extremely intelligent, and more powerful than the human mind can fathom. However, in the book of Ezekiel (28:17), it tells us that his heart became proud, and it seems that he who once was Lucifer became so impressed with his own beauty, intelligence, power, and position that he desired the glory and honor that belong to God and

God alone. What corrupted Lucifer was the sin of his self-generated pride.

In the book of Isaiah 14:14, it states that Lucifer said to himself or in his heart, "I will make myself like the Most High." So I can understand and see clearly why Lucifer fell and how he became Satan, the devil. Now please realize that it was not Lucifer alone who had to go and was cast out. No, in fact, the Bible refers to angels as stars, and it states clearly in the book of Revelation 12:4 that one-third of the angels were flung to the earth. And where do we live, beloved? So yes, they are here with us! He who once was Lucifer, now is Satan, the devil, and one-third of all God's angels live on earth in spirit form! I don't want to get off course or get sidetracked, but I do believe that it's very important to know and understand who and what we're dealing with!

I know in my heart that we, all human beings, are born into this spiritual war because of the fall of God's angels. These angels were created by God, and although they are fallen, yes, they were cast out, but they were created with gifts, abilities, skills, and talents that we really can't imagine. In fact, there are still countless creatures on land and in the sea that we haven't figured out, but we do know that there are people who have been or gotten possessed—possessed by the devil, as it's said—but it's not just he who once was Lucifer. It's all the fallen angels who are now demon spirits, demonic entities. So for me, I truly believe and know that these creatures, called fallen angels, can and do get into our minds! I also know that these fallen angels or demon spirits are the reason why the good things I want to do, I don't, and the things that I don't want to do are the things I do. Keeping in mind that it's not always that I or anyone else does things that we or I shouldn't.

So, beloved, how we can cross the chasm is by turning our hearts to the Lord, being mindful and truly thinking about the Lord, and coming to fear our God and Creator, who is truly our sustainer.

Yes, absolutely, talk to Him, thank Him, and ask for strength, grace, and guidance! Ask Him to help you humble yourself because now is the time, and today is the day, to start building the bridge to cross the chasm!

Beloved, we are all one—one people, one race, the human race created in the image of the Most High God, and when I humble myself, He lifts me up! In the book of Luke 14:11, 18:14, it states that he or she who humbles themselves will be exalted, and in the book of James 4:10, it tells us, "Humble yourself in the sight of the Lord, and He shall lift you up"!

Beloved, the laws of human nature apply to us all, and the laws of human nature tell us that a repeated action produces a habit, habits form disposition, disposition forms the will, and a rightly formed will develops character. So as we develop and form the good habit of humbling ourselves, we're building a spiritual bridge, little by little, day by day, growing closer to our heavenly Father, who is our Creator and Sustainer! Beloved, please know that the spiritual war is as real as that which our eyes can see, so please choose to humble yourself and cross the chasm with me!

Sincerely loving,
Michael T. Conklin
Your friend in this world and
brother for eternity!

ABOUT THE AUTHOR

After having experienced the trauma of his dad getting severely burned when Michael was only eleven years old, he began drinking and using drugs. At fourteen, he got expelled from school, and it was then that he was first taken to church by his aunt Gloria. Unfortunately, his aunt could only take him a couple of times, but a dear friend named Lance Tursi, who lived nearby, offered to take him, as he and his family attended the same church service that his aunt Gloria had taken him to. It was only a month or so after attending church with

Lance and his family that Michael's dad saw his devotion and began taking Michael and his two younger brothers. Michael continued to develop and build a loving relationship with the Lord, and at fifty-three years old, he reads the Bible and prays every day.